Fingerprint Analysis: Hints from Prints

by Sue Hamilton

VISIT US AT
WWW.ABDOPUBLISHING.COM

Published by ABDO Publishing Company, 8000 West 78th Street, Suite 310, Edina, Minnesota 55439.
Copyright ©2008 by Abdo Consulting Group, Inc. International copyrights reserved in all countries.
No part of this book may be reproduced in any form without written permission from the publisher.
ABDO & Daughters™ is a trademark and logo of ABDO Publishing Company.

Printed in the United States.

Editor: John Hamilton
Series Consultant: Scott Harr, J.D. Criminal Justice Dept. Chair, Concordia University St. Paul
Graphic Design: Sue Hamilton
Cover Design: Neil Klinepier
Cover Illustration: iStockphoto
Interior Photos and Illustrations: p 1 Dusting for fingerprints, iStockphoto; p 3 Fingerprint magnified, iStockphoto; p 4 Fingerprint, courtesy Bob Staupe; p 5 Print examiner, AP; p 6 Dillinger's fingerprints, AP; p 7 John Dillinger, AP; p 9 William Herschel, Photo Researchers, Inc.; p 10 Broken clay pot, iStockphoto; p 11 Mark Twain, Library of Congress; p 12 *Finger Prints* 1892 title page, courtesy Macmillan and Co.; Arch, loop, & whorl patterns, U.S. National Library of Medicine; p 13 Francis Galton, Corbis; pp 14-15 Images of fingerprint patterns, FBI; p 15 Finger pointing, Comstock; p 16 Patent and latent prints, John Hamilton; p 17 Firearm being treated for latent prints, AP; p 18 Fingerprint by millimeter ruler, iStockphoto; p 19 Instructor dusting for prints, AP; p 20 Ninhydrin-treated paper, courtesy Practice for Neurology & Diagnostics; Super Glue, John Hamilton; p 21 Chemical testing for fingerprints on a CD, Corbis; p 22 Sir Edward Henry, courtesy the Metropolitan Police of London; Sir Henry's book on classifying fingerprints, U.S. National Library of Medicine; p 23 Bonus Bureau-Fingerprint Division 1924, Library of Congress; p 24 Fingerprints, iStockphoto; p 25 Technician compares fingerprints, AP; p 26 Criminal's fingerprints are scanned into a computer database, Comstock; p 27 Glowing fingerprints, AP; p 28 Cologne spraying, iStockphoto; p 29 Testing evidence under blue light, AP, p 31 Handcuffs on fingerprint sheet, iStockphoto.

Library of Congress Cataloging-in-Publication Data

Hamilton, Sue L., 1959-
    Fingerprint analysis : hints from prints / Sue Hamilton.
       p. cm. -- (Crime scene investigation)
    Includes index.
    ISBN-13: 978-1-59928-988-5
    1. Fingerprints--Juvenile literature. 2. Fingerprints--Identification--Juvenile literature. 3. Criminal investigation--Juvenile literature. 4. Forensic sciences--Juvenile literature. I. Title.
    HV6074.H23 2008
    363.25'8--dc22
                              2007035158

CONTENTS

Fingerprints: One Of a Kind

Fingerprints can say a lot about people. The distinctive lines and swirls on the ends of our fingers reveal many facts, even giving clues about people's professions. The fingertips of guitar players are rough with calluses from pressing, plucking, and strumming the strings. On the other hand, the finger pads of tax accountants, or anyone who deals with a lot of paper, are often smooth. The paper acts like a gentle sandpaper, smoothing out the ridges on their fingers over time. Fingerprints made by people in these two professions look quite different.

Everyone's fingerprints are unique. This fact is a powerful tool used by law enforcement. Crime scene investigators often use fingerprint analysis to help solve crimes and identify criminals and sometimes even witnesses.

As a baby develops inside a mother, ridges usually begin to form on the fingers at about two months. When born, the baby will have distinct fingerprints. Even identical twins have their own fingerprint patterns. Except for accidents that result in scars, fingerprint patterns stay the same all through a person's life. Aging, weight gain, or weight loss does not alter a person's fingerprint patterns. For law enforcement agents, this is a valuable tool. While criminals may be able to change their faces with disguises or plastic surgery, they cannot change their fingerprint patterns (although some have tried).

Below: A fingerprint lifted from a vehicle. Fingerprints are a valuable forensic tool because every person's prints are unique.

Above: A police print examiner views a digital image of a fingerprint taken from a crime scene.

In the 1930s, bank robber John Dillinger was named Public Enemy Number 1 by the Federal Bureau of Investigation (FBI). To mislead the police, Dillinger tried to change his fingerprints by dipping his fingers in acid and burning off the pads. It caused him incredible pain. The result? His fingerprints grew back just as they had originally looked.

Gangster Robert Phillips had another scheme. He had the skin from his fingerprints surgically cut off, then had skin from his chest grafted onto the pads of his fingers. Since ordinary skin does not have ridges, except for the palms of the hands and soles of the feet, it seemed that this would work to disguise his fingerprints and mislead police. However, law enforcement officials don't just collect fingerprints at a crime scene. They collect as much evidence as possible, including entire footprints and handprints. Police identified Phillips' prints from the second, unaltered section of his fingers, close to his knuckles, and convicted him based on these matches.

Fingerprint analysis has grown into a detailed and important part of crime scene investigation. The FBI has more than 47 million fingerprints in its Criminal Master File database, and none of them are exactly the same. However, it is rare for a crime scene to yield a clear, perfect print.

Below: A fingerprint card from gangster John Dillinger. He was one of several gangsters who tried unsuccessfully to change their fingerprints.

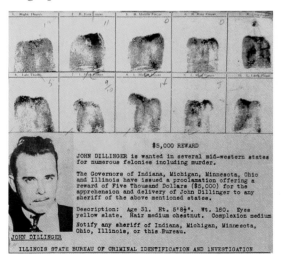

$5,000 REWARD

JOHN DILLINGER is wanted in several mid-western states for numerous felonies including murder.

The Governors of Indiana, Michigan, Minnesota, Ohio and Illinois have issued a proclamation offering a reward of Five Thousand Dollars ($5,000) for the apprehension and delivery of John Dillinger to any sheriff of the above mentioned states.

Description: Age 31. Ht. 5'8½". Wt. 160. Eyes yellow slate. Hair medium chestnut. Complexion medium

Notify any sheriff of Indiana, Michigan, Minnesota, Ohio, Illinois, or this Bureau.

JOHN DILLINGER

ILLINOIS STATE BUREAU OF CRIMINAL IDENTIFICATION AND INVESTIGATION

Today, most criminals know that their fingerprints reveal their identity. To avoid leaving fingerprints, they wear gloves. Or they carefully clean and wipe away prints from places they've touched. But criminals are often interrupted, or they may not be careful enough. Fingerprint analysts are trained to help identify the owner of even a partial print. Their work can help build and solve a case.

Left: Bank robber John Dillinger was the FBI's Public Enemy Number 1 in the 1930s. He tried to change his fingerprints by dipping his fingers in acid. The process was incredibly painful, and the fingerprints healed back as they had originally looked.

The History Of Fingerprint Analysis

Below: The contract between Sir William Herschel and Rajyadhar Konai, written in Konai's handwriting, and "signed" with his handprint.

Fingerprint analysis, also known as dactylography, is the scientific study of fingerprints for the purpose of identifying their owners. Forensics is the use of science and technology to investigate a crime and provide facts in a court of law. Fingerprint analysis became helpful to forensic scientists beginning in the 1800s.

In 1858, Sir William Herschel was a British magistrate living and working in Jungipoor, India. Herschel came up with the idea of asking a businessman to place his handprint on a contract. Herschel wanted to be sure the man would not go back on the deal.

Leaving a handprint on the contract seemed more binding than simply writing a name. Herschel continued this practice for many years. Over time, he discovered that a handprint, or even a single fingerprint, could be used to prove a person's identity.

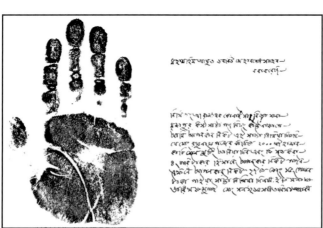

Above: Sir William J. Herschel was a British citizen living and working in India in the mid-1800s. He discovered that a handprint, or even a single fingerprint, could be used to prove a person's identity.

Above and Below: Dr. Henry Faulds saw fingerprints on ancient clay pots. He began studying prints in the 1870s.

In the 1870s, Henry Faulds was a Scottish missionary and doctor working in Japan. Faulds came across pieces of ancient clay pottery that still carried its maker's fingerprints. This fascinated Faulds, and he began to study fingerprints. In October 1880, he published an article in the British scientific journal *Nature*. He wrote, "…when bloody finger-marks or impressions on clay, glass, etc., exist, they may lead to the scientific identification of criminals." Faulds went on to tell a story about a theft that took place in a house in Tokyo, Japan. Ten fingerprints were left on a cup by the sweaty fingers of the thief. Because Faulds had collected people's fingerprints in the area, the police asked for the doctor's help to solve the crime. Faulds found an exact match with the fingerprints of a servant in another house nearby. Confronted with the evidence, the servant confessed his guilt and was arrested for robbery.

The following month, November 1880, William Herschel also published an article in *Nature* about his studies of fingerprints in India. It was the start of fingerprint analysis for use in forensic science.

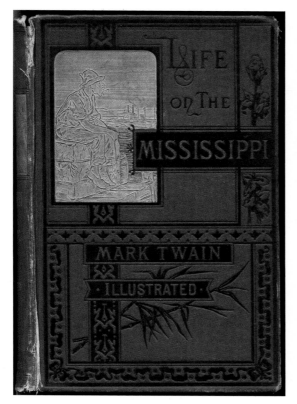

My apparatus was simple: a little red paint and a bit of white paper. I painted the ball of the client's thumb,

took a print of it on the paper, studied it that night, and revealed his fortune to him next day. What was my idea in this nonsense? It was this: When I was a youth, I knew an old Frenchman who had been a prison-keeper for thirty years, and he told me that there was one thing about a person which never changed, from the cradle to the grave — the lines in the ball of the thumb; and he said that these lines were never exactly alike in the thumbs of any two human beings. In

ON THE RIGHT TRACK.

Above: In 1882, popular author Mark Twain wrote a short story entitled *A Dying Man's Confession.* Published in Twain's 1883 book *Life on the Mississippi,* the story described the fingerprinting process, and how it could be used to identify criminals.

Not long after its discovery, the new concept of fingerprinting was brought to people's attention by popular American author Mark Twain. In 1882, Twain wrote *A Dying Man's Confession.* In the tale, a man discovers the identity of his family's killer by locating the owner of a bloody thumbprint found at the scene of the crime. Twain's fictional story was the first to bring the importance of fingerprinting to the general public. The news was out—law enforcement had an important new tool in its fight to protect the innocent and convict wrongdoers.

Above: Author Mark Twain.

Arches, Loops, and Whorls

FINGER PRINTS

BY
FRANCIS GALTON, F.R.S. ETC.

London
MACMILLAN AND CO.
AND NEW YORK
1892
All rights reserved

Building on the fingerprinting work of Henry Faulds and William Herschel, anthropologist and scientist Sir Francis Galton came up with the idea of classifying fingerprints into categories. In Galton's 1892 book, *Finger Prints*, he described three patterns for which all fingerprints may be classified: arches, loops, and whorls. These categories are still used in fingerprint analysis today.

Above: Francis Galton's 1892 book in which he described three fingerprint patterns.

Right: Samples of three fingerprint patterns: arch, loop, and whorl.

FINGER PRINTS
ARCH

FINGER PRINTS
LOOP

FINGER PRINTS
WHORL

Above: Anthropologist and scientist Sir Francis Galton came up with the idea of classifying fingerprints into three categories: arches, loops, and whorls.

Plain Arch

Tented Arch

Arches

This is a pattern where the ridges flow from one side of the finger to the other. Arches are broken down into two additional categories: plain and tented. The plain arch is the simplest of patterns, with a gentle upward curve in the middle of the finger. The tented arch has a more distinct upward flow, yielding a pattern that resembles a tent. Only about five percent of fingerprints have an arch pattern type.

Ulnar Loop

Radial Loop

Loops

Loop patterns have one or more ridges that come in on one side, make a sharp curve, and flow back out on the same side that they entered. There are two loop patterns: radial and ulnar. If the ridges of the loop flow in from the thumb side of a person's hand, that is a radial loop. If the ridges flow in from the little finger side, that is an ulnar loop. An analyst must know from which hand a print comes from—the left or the right—to decide if it is a radial or ulnar loop, since the right- and left-hand loops are opposite. Loops are the most common fingerprint pattern, making up 60 percent of all fingerprints.

Whorls

Whorls are circle-like patterns. There are four types of whorl patterns: plain, central pocket loop, double loop, and accidental. Some look like ever-growing circles, like a dartboard. Some are oval-shaped, while others are like spirals. These more complex patterns are found on about 35 percent of fingerprints.

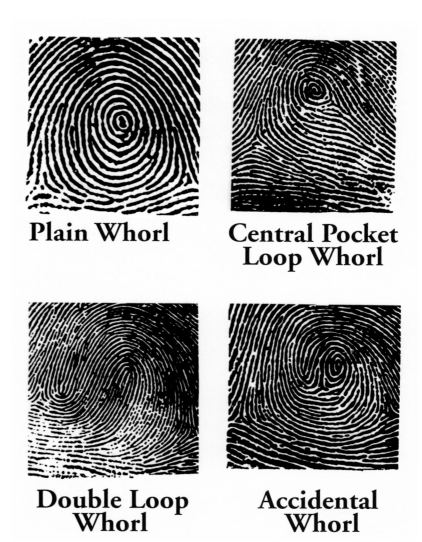

Plain Whorl

Central Pocket Loop Whorl

Double Loop Whorl

Accidental Whorl

Ridge Patterns

People tend to have similar patterns as those of their parents. This biological history, in particular a person's racial background, also plays a part in analyzing ridge patterns. For example, people of African ancestry often have arches in their fingerprint patterns, while those with European backgrounds may have loops, and many Asians have whorls.

Patent, Plastic, and Latent Prints

There are three fingerprint types that investigators are likely to find at a crime scene or on evidence: patent, plastic, or latent prints.

5-3231

Right: A patent print on an envelope. The inked print is clearly visible.

Right: A plastic print in wax.

Patent

This type of print is clearly visible. No special processing is needed to see it. Patent prints are made when blood, oil, paint, ink, dirt, or some other colored substance gets on a finger, which is then pressed onto another surface such as a counter, floor, or window.

Plastic

A plastic print is one with a three-dimensional quality. A finger's friction ridges actually show up in a soft material that retains the shape and details of the finger. A plastic print may be found in such things as butter, wax, clay, or even oil or tar. Analysts will also look for additional fingerprints underneath the ones that are clearly visible.

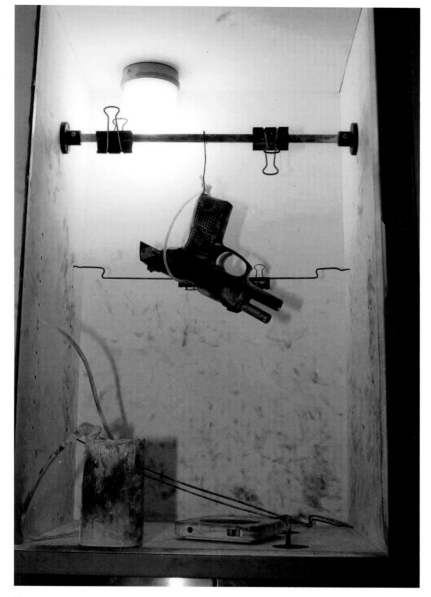

Left: A Ruger handgun hangs in a sealed box. The weapon will be exposed to fumes created by heating the chemical cyanoacrylate, commonly known as Super Glue. The chemical helps make visible any latent prints on the weapon.

Latent

A latent print needs some type of processing to make it visible. Dusting powders, chemicals, or some type of electronic process are needed to see the print. Latent prints are the most difficult type of prints to find and identify. Often only part of the print is present, and it may be blurred or twisted out of shape.

Finding and Lifting a Print

At a crime scene, or even on evidence in a forensic lab, fingerprints are often photographed. Depending on the law enforcement agency, sometimes every fingerprint found will have a picture taken. A photograph documents the exact location where a print is found. For a patent print, one that is visible, a clear photograph may be enough for an analyst to use to begin researching its owner. However, other prints must be "lifted," or "collected."

Dusting for invisible latent prints is considered an art. Fine powder particles are gently brushed onto a surface. The crime scene investigator uses a soft-bristled fingerprint brush, commonly known as a squirrel-hair brush. The delicate powder, which comes in a variety of colors, adheres to the residue left by a person's finger. However, an inexperienced investigator must be careful. Many things can go wrong. If the brushing is performed too hard, the print can be smudged and damaged. If too little powder is used, fine details will not show up. If too much powder is used, the powder can fill in the fine details and make the print unclear. Crime scene investigators often take classes in fingerprint dusting, where a gentle twirl or sweeping of the brush is taught.

Below: To record the size of a fingerprint, it is photographed next to a millimeter ruler.

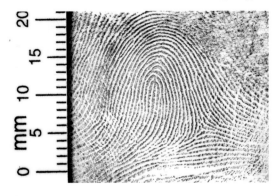

Above: Greg Dagnan, an assistant professor of criminal justice at Missouri Southern State University, demonstrates the technique for dusting fingerprints at the school's mock crime scene lab in Joplin, Missouri. Students must learn the correct technique for dusting prints without destroying them.

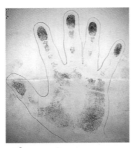

Above: A ninhydrin-treated paper shows a handprint.

Above: The chemical cyanoacrylate, commonly known as Super Glue, is used to expose fingerprints on nonporous surfaces such as glass, plastic, and metal.

Chemicals may also be used to reveal latent prints. For example, a chemical called ninhydrin is used on porous surfaces such as paper, cardboard, or raw wood. Ninhydrin reacts to the amino acids in a fingerprint. Once sprayed, the chemical will react in 10 to 20 minutes. Using a heat and humidity source, such as a steam iron, the reaction happens almost immediately. If a print is there, a purplish image will appear. This must be photographed right away because the ninhydrin will fade in a short time, making the print invisible once again.

For nonporous surfaces such as glass, plastic, and metal, a chemical called cyanoacrylate may be used. More commonly known as Super Glue, when it is heated and mixed with sodium hydroxide (another common chemical), a vapor is produced that binds to the invisible amino acids, oils, and fats of the latent fingerprint. A hard, white fingerprint becomes visible. The print can then be photographed. This technique may be completed in an airtight fuming box, or investigators may use a hand-held wand that heats a small cartridge of cyanoacrylate. The fumes are then directed at an area where a latent print may be found.

Forensic light sources also help investigators uncover latent prints. Lasers or ultraviolet lights may cause the prints to fluoresce—to glow. Often a dye stain is first applied to the prints, which make them easier to see.

Once a print is "processed," or made visible, it may be necessary to "lift" it. To lift a print, crime scene investigators use a product known as transparent lifting tape. This product is similar to household tape. One side has a sticky adhesive, and it sometimes comes in a roll. Other print lifters are sticky squares of various sizes, which may come in black or white.

Above: A CD is exposed to cyanoacrylate fuming, also known as Super Glue fuming, which reveals a number of fingerprints on the evidence.

Lifting a print is a skill learned with practice. It involves more than simply placing a piece of tape over a print. Incorrectly collected, a print may become fuzzy, especially around the edges, which might make it useless. Crime scene investigators are taught to successfully collect prints from difficult kinds of round surfaces, such as door handles, steering wheels, or light bulbs, as well as from easier flat surfaces, such as windows or mirrors.

Identifying the Owner Of a Print

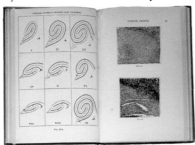

Above: Sir Edward Henry was commissioner of the Metropolitan Police of London, England, from 1903 to 1918. *Below:* Building on the work of Francis Galton, Henry invented a way to sort fingerprints to help identify criminals. It became known as the Henry Classification System.

Historically, fingerprints could only be identified by looking through hundreds of fingerprint cards and trying to find a match. This sounds impossible, but the process was greatly aided by the work of Sir Edward Henry. In 1894, Henry was the inspector general of the Bengal Police in India. After reading Francis Galton's 1892 book, *Finger Prints*, Henry became fascinated with the idea of using fingerprints in criminal investigations. Henry wrote to Galton and continued the task of classifying fingerprints.

Working with fingerprint experts Azizul Haque and Hem Chandra Bose of Calcutta, India, Henry invented a system of sorting fingerprints for use by law enforcement officials. The Henry Classification System, as it became known, assigned numbered values to all 10 of a person's fingers based on each finger's location on the hand. The system also assigned numbers to a finger's pattern type— arches, loops, or whorls. It broke them down even further into specific categories. Each fingerprint was numbered, and investigators only had to look through cards that matched that same number. There were, of course, still a large number of cards to search through.

Above: In the 1920s, thousands of fingerprint cards were organized and filed according to the Henry Classification System.

In 1901, Sir Henry returned to Great Britain. He was appointed head of the Criminal Investigation Department of Scotland Yard, the headquarters of the London Metropolitan Police. That year the Henry Classification System was put into place and the first fingerprint bureau was set up at Scotland Yard. Soon after, the system began being used by countries around the world, including the United States. By 1904, the National Bureau of Criminal Identification had been established in America, containing the country's first fingerprint repository. Later renamed the International Association for Identification (IAI), the science of fingerprinting was here to stay.

Today, once a print has been lifted or photographed, the image is scanned into a computer system. A search is then conducted through the Automated Fingerprint Identification System (AFIS), or the FBI's Integrated Automated Fingerprint Identification System (IAFIS). AFIS is a database of known prints. IAFIS is a database that includes index-finger prints, as well as "tenprints"—a scan of all 10 fingers of a person. These prints are largely from criminals, but also may have come from military service members, or from people providing fingerprints for background checks for certain jobs, such as people who work in law enforcement, schools, or with hazardous materials.

When an unknown print is sent to AFIS or IAFIS, the computer searches through millions of fingerprint records, comparing certain points on the print. The computer may find one or several prints with similar characteristics. When an analyst thinks there's been a match, he or she will then look at the actual fingerprint record. The fingerprint analyst will determine if the crime scene print matches that individual's print.

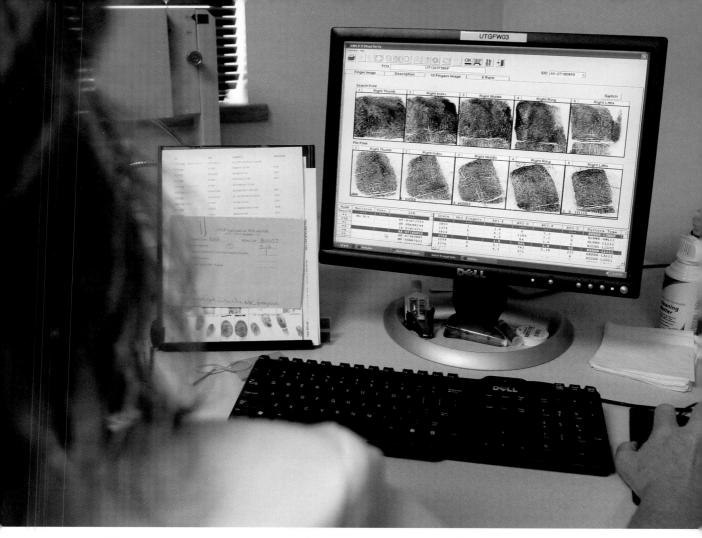

Above: A technician compares fingerprints with possible matches in the criminal system at the Bureau of Criminal Identification (BCI) headquarters in Kearns, Utah. In 2004, the BCI ran 31,841 fingerprint checks. In 2006, that number jumped to nearly 52,000. The agency expects that requests for fingerprint checks will continue to grow significantly over the next several years.

As with any process that involves people, fingerprint analysis is not a perfect science. There is always a chance of human error occurring. Although mistakes do happen, there is no doubt that law enforcement officials find fingerprint analysis an excellent tool in crime scene investigations.

The Future Of Fingerprinting

While there are millions of people's fingerprints on record, there are many millions more people whose fingerprints have never been taken. If a fingerprint is lifted, but no match is found, what good is it? Sometimes, quite a bit.

A fingerprint often contains a mixture of skin cells, sweat, and sometimes other substances from places the person has been. Researchers have discovered that the trace amounts of sweat contain many clues about the print's owner.

Scientists have been able to tell the difference between the fingerprints of smokers and nonsmokers. They do this by testing for cotinine, a substance formed after a smoker's body absorbs nicotine, the addictive drug found in cigarettes. Why cotinine instead of nicotine? Nonsmokers may test positive for nicotine just because they have been in contact with smokers. Cotinine only shows up when people have actually brought nicotine into their bodies.

One test makes it even easier to tell if the owner of the print is a smoker or nonsmoker. It's been discovered that the ridge patterns on smokers' fingerprints glow when treated with a special fluorescent dye. Nonsmokers' prints do not glow.

Below: Today, law enforcement officials often scan criminals' fingerprints directly into a computer database.

Above: Once invisible, some fingerprints glow in special light.

Above: Scientists have discovered that trace amounts of sweat left by fingerprints can be tested to determine if a suspect smokes, what ethnic foods he or she eats, and even what aftershave, perfume, or hair care products a person uses.

Knowing whether a suspect or witness is a smoker or nonsmoker is a great clue for detectives working on a case, but a fingerprint may provide them with even more information. The trace amounts of sweat may also be tested to reveal if a person is taking illegal drugs or legal medications.

On a more detailed level, tests are being conducted to find out such things as what kind of cosmetics and hair products people use, based on their fingerprint residue. Dr. Sue Jickells, a scientist and chemist at Kings College in London, England, stated, "In one sample we picked up some hair product that was eventually linked back to one of our students." They may also be able to tell what aftershave a person uses. Jickells said, "For about five hours after application, aftershave is also left behind." Although researchers cannot yet pinpoint exact products, Jickells states, "But I think in the future biosensors will be used to easily tell them apart."

Fingerprints may yield even more secrets about people's habits. Studies are being conducted to find out what kinds of foods and drinks people consume. If it's discovered that a suspect eats certain types of ethnic foods and drinks a great deal of coffee, investigators may have a clue where to begin looking for the person. The more fingerprint secrets that can be uncovered, the greater the chances law enforcement agents have of understanding and solving criminal cases.

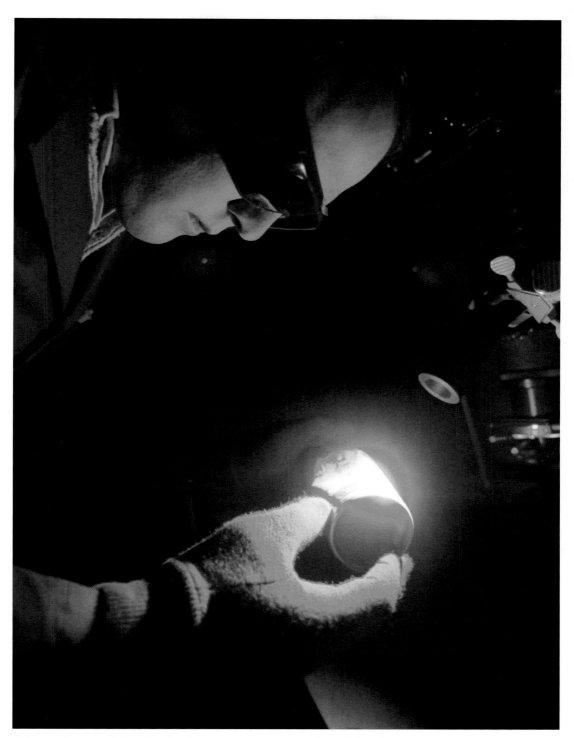

Above: A technician looks for fingerprints under a blue light.

GLOSSARY

AMINO ACIDS — The basic building blocks of protein found in humans and plants. There are 20 naturally occurring amino acids.

ANTHROPOLOGIST — A person who studies all areas of human life, including origins, history, behavior, speech, religion, as well as physical, social, and cultural development.

BIOSENSOR — A device that detects life processes (such as heart beats) or chemicals in living creatures.

CHEMIST — A person who is an expert in chemistry. Chemistry is a science that identifies the substances that make up various materials.

CRIMINOLOGIST — A person who studies crimes and criminals to understand how these people think and behave. A criminologist's work helps law enforcement find and capture criminals by predicting what a criminal may do in certain situations.

EVIDENCE — Objects, and sometimes information, that helps prove the details and facts in a legal investigation.

FBI — The Federal Bureau of Investigation (FBI) is a division of the United States Justice Department responsible for enforcing federal laws.

MAGISTRATE — A judge or other public officer with the power to enforce the laws of an area and decide cases brought before a court of justice.

MARK TWAIN — An American author who lived from 1835 to 1910. He wrote such classic tales as *The Adventures of Tom Sawyer, Huckleberry Finn,* and *Life on the Mississippi*. His real name was Samuel Langhorne Clemens. He once worked as a riverboat pilot on the Mississippi River. His pseudonym, or fictional name, was Mark Twain. It is a riverboat term that describes a water depth of two fathoms. A fathom is equal to 6 feet (1.8 m).

Nonporous — A substance or object that has no pores, and thus does not allow gas or liquid to travel through the material. Examples of nonporous materials include glass, plastic, and some metals and rocks.

Pathologist — A person who studies diseases and how they affect human bodies at different stages.

Perpetrator — A person who commits a crime.

Porous — An object or substance that is full of pores, allowing gasses and liquids to pass through. Examples of some porous materials include wood, clay, and concrete.

Repository — A building, location, or container where things are stored.

Scar — A usually permanent mark left on the skin of a human or animal after a wound has healed.

Trace Evidence — A small, but measurable, amount of evidence. It can be anything from sweat in a fingerprint, to a small amount of drugs or explosives, to a tiny drop of blood.

INDEX